Don't Set Limits on
GOD

Lora Fulp Efaw, M.D.

ISBN 978-1-63844-518-0 (paperback)
ISBN 978-1-63844-519-7 (digital)

Christian Faith Publishing, Inc.
832 Park Avenue
Meadville, PA 16335
www.christianfaithpublishing.com

Printed in the United States of America

PREFACE

One of my earliest childhood memories was flipping through (and sometimes scribbling in) my mother's many journals. When I asked her what they were, she would tell me that God was telling her to write her story. Throughout my childhood and even into my adult years, she would continue to update me whenever God revealed to her what the next chapter was going to be called and what it was going to entail. I never understood the severity of my mother's health conditions until I was a bit older, but I knew my mom meant a great deal to a lot of people in her life. People would tell me how much my mom meant to them, how as a physician she had helped them in their lives, and how she was a survivor. So it's not hard to believe that I grew up thinking my mom was a superhero.

My mother has always been my biggest inspiration in life. She has encouraged and supported me through the toughest times in my life—not just by her words and actions but through her journey. She has been through hell and back, but she always keeps her faith. When I ask her how she does it, she always reminds me of the story Job in the Bible. Job's entire life was snatched right out of his hands. His world was turned upside down. Everything was taken from him—his land, his resources, and even his own children! He was plagued with sickness and disease and fell into a deep depression. He lamented day and night. He prayed and cried out to God in his time of need, and in the end, God gave him back everything that was taken from him—and then some! He never blamed God for his troubles, but he leaned on God in his time of need and praised God in his triumph. This story always inspires me, not just in my own life but in my mom's life as well. There were so many times when we thought, *When will this end? Why is this happening? What are we going to do?*

Even though it's been difficult, my mom has always kept a positive attitude and never for a second thought that God had abandoned her. She believes in her healing. She believes in God's power, and it has given her an unimaginable amount of strength and courage. One of the greatest skills she has taught me in life is the power of positive words of affirmation. I used to say the most horrible things to and about myself. Over time, I realized the negative impact. If anyone else was saying those things to me, it would be so harmful and damaging, so why was I saying it about myself and my own life? Once I started changing my words and speaking blessings over myself and others, I began to change. I became happier and started accomplishing things that I didn't even think were possible!

My mom continues to speak her blessings into existence, and I believe it is why she is here today. Her faith and her strength are a big part of her, but they are not entirely her own. She leans on God and relies on Him to carry her through her toughest struggles. He has given her an unbelievable amount of strength and courage. He has deeply and truly blessed all of us with my mother. I am so grateful to have her in my life. She is a blessing to everyone she meets. She inspires me every day to be a better person. Her journey has motivated and inspired me to look up, have faith, and fight back when life tries to tear me down. My hope in her sharing her story is that it will help others the way it has helped me. My prayer for this book is that you, too, will lean on God in your time of need and let Him guide you and give you the strength He has given her throughout her entire life. My mom's faith has kept her shining in her darkest places. She encourages me every day to have faith, fight the good fight, and finish the race.

Olivia Efaw

But those who hope in the Lord will renew
their strength. They will soar on wings
like eagles; they will run and not grow
weary, they will walk and not be faint.
—Isaiah 40:31 NIV

1

My Story

I feel compelled by God to tell my story. I have had many trials in my life but always have found that my God has been faithful through each one. He has carried me through every time and has brought good from each trial the enemy sent to destroy me. I have had many supernatural experiences. Some of these things may seem strange to some, but I pray that you will know the truth and reality of each one. I believe since God is supernatural, we as His children should expect to have supernatural experiences. It is my prayer that in reading this, you are blessed in some way or ministered to by the Holy Spirit.

I hope this book changes lives.

I grew up in a small town. I gave my heart to Jesus at ten years of age in a small country church during a revival. I remember the feeling as if it was yesterday. We were singing an invitation hymn called "Just as I Am." I felt a longing inside of me and a feeling as if my heart was racing. I felt beckoned to give my life to God. I had a sense of relief when my sister stepped out into the aisle to walk forward. She gave me the courage to do the same. I remember the sense of elation and relief I felt as I walked to the front of the church and told the minister I wanted to be saved. I began to learn more about my God, and I had a longing to do the things He had for me to do in my life.

When I was a teenager, some things happened in the church that gravely disappointed me. Some of the elders in the church felt that the pastor was too close with a few of the members of the congregation, one of whom was me. They asked him to leave the church. I could not understand how these people who were family to me could do this. I thought at the time, *If this is what church is all about, I want nothing to do with it.* At this point, I turned my back on the church and went my own way.

I was in college at the time, and I had goals to work toward. I graduated from college with a bachelor's degree in biology and then went to medical school. I was very busy with my studies and made little time for God. I prayed and sometimes read my Bible. I rarely attended church. Mostly, I would just ask God for help when I was in a difficult situation. Even though I gave very little of my time to God, He was always there when I needed Him to carry me through a difficult situation.

I knew in my heart that I was doing what God had called me to do. I joined the Navy in medical school. They offered me a scholarship which paid my tuition, books, and medical supplies and also gave me money to pay my living expenses. This was a great blessing as my parents were trying to help me and my brother who was also in college. I graduated from medical school and did my internship and residency in a naval hospital. After residency, I was in the navy for an additional three years. At my particular duty station, most of my patients were retirees. I began to take notice of two things about my patients: A lot of the patients without children were very lonely. Those with children and grandchildren were healthier and more vibrant. These patients were on very little medication, and they took nutritional supplements. I began to think more about my future and knew that I wanted children. I began to have conversations with my husband on our evening walks. At first, he was against the idea. He felt like he had not accomplished the things he wanted in life and was not ready for a family. I would determine not to speak of it again but found I could not help myself. I kept bringing up the idea. After spending a weekend with his friend who has a child, my husband finally agreed we should try to have a baby. His friend had shared with him how he loved being a father.

I was twenty-five when we married, and we had been married for seven years. I knew that being older and having kids carried more risks and wanted to have children before the age of thirty-five. A month later, I found out that I was pregnant, and eight months later, we had twin girls. After our daughters were born, I decided to leave the Navy. I could not stand the thought of possibly being away from my daughters for deployment. My family wanted us to be closer to them. We moved to a new town close to our family and started new jobs. I was busy with work and my family and still had made little to no time for God in my life.

One day when my daughters were twenty months old, I was sitting in the floor playing with them, and death hit me like a ton of bricks. This feeling came out of the blue. I knew in an instant that I was dying and that I would not live long enough for the girls to remember me. I knew they would be well cared for by other family members, but I knew no one could care for them like I could. I began to sob. Over the next few days and weeks, I would wonder how it would happen. Would I have a wreck? I was healthy as far as I knew, so I never thought about illness. I went to a medical conference soon after this. I had thought about not going to the conference because of this overwhelming feeling I was going to die. But I thought, *If it's my time to die, it's my time, and there is nothing I can do about it.* I went to my hotel room after the conference every evening and stared at the walls wondering how I was going to die. I cried almost the entire drive home, and when I arrived home alive, I fell on my knees on my kitchen floor and cried again. I just could not believe I was still alive. That is how strong this feeling was. In the next few weeks, I had several experiences. I had a dream that I died. I also had an experience in which I felt a presence in the doorway of my bedroom and heard evil laughter. The presence came over to me and touched me on my finger. It felt like a skeleton finger touched me. I know that sounds strange. It was very eerie to me.

About a month later, it was time for the holidays. Thanksgiving and Christmas came and went, but throughout the entire time, I knew I needed to make the most of this time because it would be my last. When we returned from visiting family for the holidays, I called one of my friends who was an internist and told her I needed her to examine me and tell me that everything was okay. I told her of the strange feeling of death that I could not shake. I went to her office, and upon examining me, she found a mass on my cervix. She was uncertain what this was and recommended I see my gynecologist. I had seen my gynecologist earlier that year and had a completely normal exam. The next week, I saw my gynecologist, and the mass had doubled in size. It was the size of a tangerine. It was growing very fast. She was able to obtain some tissue from the mass which she sent to pathology and would call me a few days later with the diagnosis. I took a couple of days off from work. I told my office manager I needed some personal time. My family knew I had been to the doctor and had some tests. I did not tell anyone that I had cancer, but I knew this was going to be the diagnosis. I knew as large as the mass was, the prognosis was not good.

The next night, one of the twins awakened and was crying. I went and picked her up and carried her to the rocking chair. As I sat there rocking her in the middle of the night, I hit the power button on the TV remote. When the television came on, there was a preacher speaking.

He said, "I do not know what your problem is, but nothing is too big for God. Whatever your problem is, I want you to turn it over to God. And do you know what He will say? He will say, 'It's no problem at all.' And when you give your problem to God, He will give you instant peace."

Then he said, "I don't want you to feel guilty about coming to God in your time of need. That's how we all come to Him."

Well, he just described exactly how I was feeling. I immediately knew this man was talking to me. I said, *Okay, God, this is one problem that Lora cannot handle on her own.* (This was a statement coming from a very independent woman. As a young girl even, I always wanted to do things for myself. I was a person who did not think she needed others to help her, and I found it difficult to take their help. I am in the business of helping others. I solve my own problems and the problems of others daily.) I gave this problem to God, and instantly I felt a peace that I could not explain. I did not know what was going to happen or what I would have to endure, but I knew He would carry me through. I knew He could handle this. I went back to sleep, and when I awakened, I began to wait for the phone call from my doctor.

Early that morning, the phone rang, and it was my mother. All she knew was that I had been to the doctor and had some tests and was waiting on the results. She asked if I wanted her to come over, and I said yes. Without asking any more questions, she was on her way. A while later, I received the call from the doctor.

She said, "Lora, I have some news, and it is not good."

I said, "It's okay. I know. Go ahead and tell me."

She said that she usually did not give results like this over the phone, but she told me that I had cancer of the cervix. This was on a Friday. She referred me to a specialist who would see me on Monday morning and operate that afternoon. I cannot explain the peace that I felt. It was overwhelming. I hung up the phone and turned to my mother and did one of the hardest things I have ever had to do. I told her that I had cancer. Then, she did one of the hardest things she had ever had to do and picked up the phone and called my dad.

God was taking care of the details even at this time. My aunt and uncle had stopped by my dad's store and were with him when my mother told him his daughter had cancer. I am so grateful that God ensured he was not alone for this. My mother began calling everyone she knew, and prayer chains began for me that day. As the day progressed, so did my peace.

Later that day, my brother and his family came, and we spent time talking about my living will and ensuring I had things in order. My brother is a lawyer. As the day progressed, I began to feel more people praying for me. I had a stillness inside of me and had no fear.

When my brother was ready to leave, he asked if we could pray. I said sure. My husband, mother, father, brother, sister-in-law, and I stood in a circle holding hands. I was holding one of the twins, and my mother was holding the other.

My brother said, "Our Father, who art in heaven—" and both of the girls began to scream.

My sister-in-law took the girls into another room. We joined hands again, and my brother began to pray.

"Father, you tell us wherever two or more are gathered together, there you will be also."

I fell back onto the floor, and a flood of electricity was racing through my body. My family was asking if I was okay, but I could not speak.

My mom, who was kneeling beside me said, "She's okay. It's Jesus!"

A few minutes later, I was able to sit up; and when I did, I opened my eyes and started laughing this uncontrollable laughter. It was at this moment that the death left me, and it has never returned. I did not know what I may have to go through, but I knew I was no longer going to die. They helped me up, and we sat on the sofa. Every time I started to talk, all I could do was laugh as if I were drunk.

My brother began to pray again. "Father, if this is you…"

I knew it was God!

I went to bed that night and began to pray. As I prayed, I saw a picture of a man. I did not know his name, but I had seen him before. We had visited a neighbor's church, and he was their pastor. I heard God speak to me in that still small voice.

He said, *This is a good man with a good heart. You go to him and ask him to pray with you.*

Well, I had not planned on going to church that Sunday. I had to do a bowel prep to prepare for surgery and drive over three hours to get to this doctor's office. I needed my rest also, right? But I was going to do what I heard God say. I told my family on Saturday that I was going to church, and they said they would go with me.

When I went to the church, the preacher spoke on prayer.

At the end of the service, he said, "Now this is why you have come here today."

Okay, this was another preacher whom I knew was speaking to me. I wondered if there was a blue light flashing over my head or something. But I did not hesitate when the music played. I walked to the front of the church and told this man that God told me to ask him to pray for me. I told him a little about my situation and that I had to leave that day to drive to another city for surgery the following day. He and the entire congregation prayed for me. So many came to me and said they sensed a peace about me and knew things were going to be okay.

After prayer, the pastor asked me if I wanted him to drive to the hospital and be with me and my family for the surgery. I said that I did. Well, God said he was a good man! He drove over three hours and prayed with me before surgery and sat with my family during a very long surgery. I will never forget him or what he did for me and my family. He did not know me. I was not a member of his church. He certainly did not have to be at the hospital with us and certainly not three hours from home. He was obedient to God, and I am forever grateful. I knew the workers in the hospital were praying for me also. The lab tech who drew my blood and the orderly who wheeled me to the operating room prayed for me. They did not say anything, but I knew.

I made it through surgery, and it was a few days after that we found out the pathology results. This was a very aggressive tumor. But it had not spread, and the surgeon was able to get all of the cancer. The postoperative period was not easy, but God was with me and gave me the strength to get through.

After recovering from the surgery, my doctor made the recommendation for radiation. I was not going to do the radiation unless I had peace from God. Three months later, my dad had a heart attack. It was a blockage proximal in the left anterior descending artery of his heart, just as it branched off the left main artery (the widow-maker). Well, God spared my dad's life, and it was at that time that I knew I had to do the radiation. My dad was so worried about me, and I understood how he felt after coming so close to losing him. I started the radiation, and my radiation oncologist had me see an oncologist who recommended intravenous chemotherapy along with the radiation for six weeks. After I finished this treatment, I had to go into the hospital again for a special type of radiation called brachytherapy. The night before going back into the hospital, I had a dream that my papa, who passed away when I was in medical school, was driving me in his pickup truck down a dirt road. I looked over into a pasture and saw rows and rows of clouds hovering over the ground as far as I could see. There were too many to count. They were all in the shape of praying hands. I knew this was God's way of telling me many people were praying and I was going to be okay.

This radiation procedure required going back to the operating room for a device to be placed in my body which would house the radiation for five days. I would have to lie flat on my back for that entire time and could only have very limited visitation due to the radiation. It was dangerous for others to be exposed to this radiation. The morning I was to go to the operating room for the procedure, I was lying in bed praying with my eyes closed, and I heard my cousin who lived three hours away praying as if she were right beside my bed. It was clear she was praying for me regarding what I was about to endure. I believe that was God's way of reassuring me that morning. This was a horrible experience, but I endured this treatment with God's amazing grace. I was done with this cancer and all the treatment and was grateful for what God had brought me through.

The recovery from chemotherapy and radiation is not instant. It takes years for the body to recover from the damage. The negative effects of the radiation are worse after many years. This is something most people do not understand. God, however, is always there to strengthen and encourage us through these difficult times.

One night during my recovery period, I had a dream that my uncle who passed away when I was in high school came to me and was pushing me in a swing. He asked how I was doing and said he just came to check on me. I told him I was doing okay. We talked for a while, and then he said he had to go. We hugged, and I remember not wanting to let go. Then I felt as if we were torn apart from one another, and he was gone.

One morning, I saw an angel standing in my bedroom. She did not have wings, but I knew she was an angel. She was wearing a beautiful, ornate dress, and she had curly hair. She did not speak. She just stood there looking at me for a few moments, and then she was gone. I felt peace from her presence.

About five to six months after I completed the treatment for the cancer, I found a lump in my breast. Notice I said *the* cancer, not *my* cancer. I believe strongly in the power of what we speak and that we have what we say we have. The cancer is not mine and has never been mine. It does not belong to me or in me. I am not denying its existence. I am simply denying its right to exist in my body. I am a child of God, and by the stripes of Jesus, I am healed. I believe the Word of God is truth and His truth can change the facts.

My first thought was that there was no way I could have two cancers in one year. But I called the doctor and had a mammogram and biopsy which revealed invasive cancer of the breast. I underwent a lumpectomy, and the doctors recommended chemotherapy and radiation. I started the chemotherapy and became very ill. I could not eat or drink, and I had to keep going to the hospital for intravenous fluids to keep me hydrated. I could not hold my head up off the pillow. I lost my hair within a couple of weeks. The treatments were every three weeks. After the first round of chemotherapy, I thought I would die and was certain I could not do another cycle. By the time the next cycle was due, my white blood cell count was too low, and we had to postpone the treatment for a week. I thought I could do another cycle, but again I became even more ill with the second round of chemotherapy. I was going to the hospital daily for intravenous fluids. I became even weaker. I felt like I was dying.

I started praying and asking God if I was in His will. I felt that if I was in His will, He would carry me through. I prayed, *Lord, am I doing what is in Your will? Or am I putting my trust in the medical doctors and doing what they want me to do?*

The following Sunday afternoon, I went to my room for some quiet time. I began watching a video of gospel singing that my pastor had given to me. As I was listening to the music, I heard "Mark 2:11." I was not sure if this was even a scripture. I took my Bible from the nightstand and opened it to Mark 2:11. I read "I tell you, get up, take up your mat and go home." This was the scripture in which the paralyzed man was healed. These words were spoken to him by Jesus. I thought, *God, are you telling me to stop this chemotherapy and go on with my life?* I could not be sure. I called a pastor who had been praying for me. He wanted to meet with me. We scheduled a time to meet at the hospital. He told me he felt like I was going to get a visitation. I was not sure what that meant. He prayed for me, and we hung up. That night, I could not sleep. I got up and went downstairs to the sofa. I was lying there with my eyes closed, and suddenly the presence of Jesus was in the room. I did not see Him visually, but I knew his presence was in the room. I knew it was Him just as I would know my closest family when they walk into the room. He bent over and took my face into His hands and kissed me on the forehead. Then He was gone. I got up and went to bed. The next morning, I told my husband what had happened and asked him if he thought I was crazy. He said that he just thought my faith in God was that strong and I was not crazy.

A couple of days later, I met with the pastor and another couple at the hospital. We went into the chapel, and I shared with them a little about what I had been going through. The pastor asked if he could pray, and I said yes. We stood up. The pastor stood in front of me, and the couple stood behind me. He told me to lift my hands and close my eyes and focus on Jesus on the cross because that is the source. I did as he asked, and he began to pray. As he prayed, I fell back onto the floor. The man and woman behind me caught me and helped me to the floor safely. My arms and legs began to shake uncontrollably. I shook for a long time, and then I started laughing uncontrollably. I laughed so long and so hard. It was that kind of belly laughter you have when you are a child. When the laughter stopped, I felt someone take my arms over my head and someone took my feet, and I felt like I was being stretched. I opened my eyes. The pastor asked me if I saw or heard anything. I said no. He asked if I knew I was laughing. I said yes. The pastor and the couple were sitting on the chapel pews. The woman said she saw beads of oil appearing in my hands as they were stretched over my head. She said that was healing. As we were talking, I closed my eyes again, and the presence of Jesus was in the room. I knew it was Him just as I would know my dad when he walked into the room.

Right away I said, *Oh, Jesus, what do I do about the chemo? What about the radiation? What about the tamoxifen?*

Tamoxifen is a drug that the doctors wanted me to take for five years to help prevent recurrence of the cancer. Jesus was silent.

I said, *Oh, Jesus, I am so sorry. I know you will tell me in your own time when you are ready. I totally submit to your will.*

My hands dropped by my sides. Then he started talking. He was just waiting for my total submission.

He told me about the chemo, *No, do not take it*. About the radiation, He said, *No, do not do it*. About the tamoxifen, He said, *No, do not take it*. He said, *By my stripes, you are healed. No more doubts*.

I had been struggling with doubt. Having two cancers in one year had caused me to doubt my faith. He talked to me about many things. He told me things I needed to hear. He told me that the chemotherapy and radiation had done a lot of damage to my body. He would take care of that also, and it would be as if nothing was ever there. He told me that my physical healing was not the most important thing. He said the fact that He died on the cross and is alive today is the message He wants me to share with others. My Redeemer lives! This is the most important thing. He talked with me about my husband and my children. He told me that I am precious and He loves me. I told Him that I love Him. He said that I do not have to do anything for Him to love me. I have always been a performer, and somehow I felt that I had to do good things to earn love. I was an excellent student in school. I was valedictorian of my high school. By getting good grades, I received attention and approval. I mistakenly equated this attention and approval with love. Jesus took this lie from me and revealed His truth. I do not have to do anything to earn His love. He loves me just the way I am. Love is a free gift; it cannot be earned.

After this, I could not hear Him any longer, but He was still talking. I was nodding my head up and down. I was saying, *Yes, sir. Yes, sir. Yes, sir. Yes, sir. Yes, sir*. This went on for a long time. At one point, I was patting my cheeks saying *Me? Me?* It was as if I could not believe He would choose me. What I feel about this part is that Jesus was speaking to my spirit. He was telling me things He wants me to do, and I was agreeing. He was telling me things my mind was not ready to hear yet, but my spirit knows everything He said. In time, I believe my mind will know everything that I have agreed to with Jesus. I am certain that I will do everything He told me to do.

When He started to leave, I said, *Jesus, please stay. Don't leave me*.

He said, *Lora, I cannot stay with you like this. But you know that I will never leave you and I will never forsake you. I will be with you always.*

I said, *I know.*

As He was talking to me, every time He said "You know," it was something from the Bible.

As He left, He said, *Now you praise me!*

My hands went straight up in the air, and I began to say, *Praise you, Jesus. Praise you, Jesus.*

I was praising Him as never before with my whole being. Over and over again, I was saying "Praise you, Jesus." Then I began to speak another language and then another language and then another. There were several different languages. I do not speak any other language except English, but I could tell when I was speaking a different language by the change in dialect. I know that my "Praise you, Jesus" was not adequate for what my Lord deserves, and I believe the Holy Spirit took over to give Jesus the praise He deserves. After this, I started shaking uncontrollably. When I finally opened my eyes and got up off the floor, it had been two hours. I felt great. I thanked the pastor and the couple for their time and prayer and then went home to my family.

The next day I went to the oncology clinic for my blood draw. My white blood cell count had been very low from the chemotherapy, and they were monitoring this closely. I told them before they drew my blood that my counts were up. They said to let them draw my blood, and we would wait and see. I told them to go ahead and draw my blood. I said that I was going to work and they could call me with the result. They asked if I would come back if my counts were low, and I agreed, knowing I would not have to go back. A short while later, the nurse called me at work and said that I was right; my counts were up by about ten thousand. I told my doctors that I was not going to continue the chemotherapy. I did not do the radiation or take the medication. I obeyed Jesus. I believe that if I had continued the treatment at that time, I would not be alive today. My body had not recovered from the previous treatment six months earlier and was very toxic. My body could not tolerate any more.

About two years later, I was ironing one day, and I had a vision of a building. This was a healing place. A place where people could come for healing of the soul and body. So often, the medical community focuses on our physical being without addressing the spirit or soul. I believe we are spiritual beings in a physical body and we have a soul. It is the wounds of the soul that give rise to a lot of the physical disease people suffer. I saw the outside of the building and then the inside. I saw a room for spiritual counseling. God let me know this was the most important. I saw medical examination rooms and an area for nutritional supplements. There were multiple healing modalities all in this one place. I saw the people go into the spiritual counseling room first and then from there to other parts of the center as needed. I saw all of these things working together to bring about healing. I knew this was a place God wanted me to develop. I was tired of doing Band-Aid medicine where doctors give a pill for every ailment. I wanted to see people walk in wellness instead of taking multiple pills for multiple symptoms and not getting better.

I began making plans to transition from my current position as an employee of the hospital to owning my own practice. On April 15, 2002, I opened the Center for Healing and Wellness. It was not easy. There were a lot of sacrifices required. I cut my salary to about one-third of what I was making. There were a lot of long days and nights.

One night a few months after we had opened the center, I awakened and felt frightened. I woke my husband and asked him to hold me and told him the devil was trying to steal my healing. I had been to my doctors about six weeks prior to this with a clear checkup. A couple of days later, I found a lump in my breast. It was cancer again. I underwent surgery to remove the tumor. With this recurrence of the cancer, my doctors did not recommend chemotherapy. My radiation oncologist however said if I did not do the radiation, he would lay himself in front of my car, and I could run over him. I went through the radiation for six weeks daily, Monday through Friday. God carried me through this time, and a good friend drove me an hour to and from the hospital for my treatment every day. I was able to continue working through the treatment time with no complications except decreased energy.

This was a critical time in my life. I was under a lot of stress with starting this new practice. It was something I know the devil did not want. In my practice, we pray for patients and strive to help them heal.

I again walked in this healing for eight years. I had built a new office building, and we had just moved into this new office when I found another lump in my breast. I had just been through two of the most stressful years of my life with some family issues.

My father-in-law was diagnosed with lung cancer, and after taking five different chemotherapy drugs, none of them had worked. His doctor told him there was nothing more that could be done. He stopped all treatment in January 2009, and we knew he did not have much longer to live. My husband was in denial. His dad was his best friend. They were very close.

In February of 2009, my husband went on a vacation with his friend on Valentine's Day weekend. Shortly thereafter, I had a dream. In the dream I was running down a dirt road. Cancer had attacked my spine. As I was running down the road, I was proclaiming God's Word as truth and the cancer as a lie. I was proclaiming my healing and quoting scripture as loud as I could. I shared this dream with my sister. She shared this with a woman she knew who interprets dreams. This lady said that cancer is not cancer in the dream. It is something that is going to come up and attack me from behind. I will not see it coming. It is meant to destroy me, but it will not succeed because I am running in the dream. I knew this was a warning from God.

A couple of weeks later, I discovered my husband had met someone on that weekend trip with his friend. He was having an affair. I was devastated. Needless to say, I did not see this coming. I knew whatever the dream was about would be something that was meant to knock me off my feet, but never did I think it would be this. I felt like someone had taken my soul and ripped it in half. I had a dagger in my heart. We separated, and he moved out of our home. I went to counseling, and over the next six months, I had come to terms with this life-changing event. I knew it was not my fault. I think it is human to always feel that when something like this happens, there must be something wrong with you or something you did or neglected.

I realized through counseling that the affair was not about me and it was not something I caused to happen. It was something my husband chose to do. It was amazing how God carried me through this difficult time and strengthened me. Oh, I cried in my shower and almost every night. But day after day, I was able to get up, get dressed, and go to work. I began to focus on me and started taking better care of myself. I was determined that I would not look defeated even if I felt that way. This was a difficult road in my life journey, but I was determined that I was going to look as good as I could as I went through this. God was faithful to daily give me little "pats on the back." I received so many compliments. People would say that I never looked better or how beautiful I looked. I remember a doctor stopping me outside the hospital one morning. He said that he did not know what all I was going through, but he wanted me to know that I was a strong person. He said that I offer a unique approach to medicine in this community and that he felt what I had to offer was very special. I knew this was another pat on the back from my Father. I thanked him, and when I got into my car to go to my office, I cried tears of gratefulness. He will never know how much his kind words meant to me or how deeply they touched my heart.

During this time, God taught me how to lift myself up daily without depending on others. Sometimes we may have others to help carry us through a battle; other times it is just God and us. Don't get me wrong. I had many friends and family to support me through this time, and I am grateful for them. But God showed me that I can sometimes go straight to Him and He is always the lifter upper of my head. I would cry out to God when I was in my car driving alone. At first when I was so angry at my husband, I told God that I would not mind if He wanted to put a hot branding iron to my husband's heart because I had a dagger in mine. I even offered to help. I told God just how I felt. He already knew what was in my heart anyway. Then one night, I was lying in my bed, and I began to pray. I poured out my heart to Jesus. I asked for forgiveness for all the hurt, resentment, betrayal, bitterness, and hate I was carrying. I did not want it any longer.

I cried out to Jesus most of that night and gave Him all of my junk. I gave Him all of my anger regarding what my children were going through. I asked the Holy Spirit to help me forgive my husband completely. I also forgave the woman with whom my husband had the affair. I let it all go, and Jesus was there to take every bit of it from me. The next day, my cousin called. She said that she usually did not have visions, but she was awakened in the night and saw me on my knees before Jesus. His hand was on my head. She said I had one daughter to my left and the other daughter on my right side and there was a circle of angels surrounding us. At that point, God began to heal my heart. One morning not long after, I awoke; and as I was still lying in bed, I saw my heart in God's hands. He had a needle and thread and was sewing my torn heart. The healing was a process, and it was something I had to walk out daily. The feelings of hurt and bitterness would try to come back over and over for a time.

As these feelings came, I would tell God that I will forgive my husband, and I asked the Holy Spirit to help me. This was something I could not accomplish on my own. There was a song that was popular at that time on Christian radio called "Walking Her Home" by Mark Schultz. It was about a young man who one day walked a girl home from school and held her hand. The song was about their journey and how he was always there for her, holding her hand through their life as they married and had children. Then the song talks about her getting ill and going into the nursing home. On the night she died, he was there at the nursing home, holding her hand till the end.

I heard that song and began to cry out to Jesus, *I need a man like that! Please give me a man like that. That is what I need.*

Well, about a week later, I was driving in my car; and that song came to my mind.

Then I heard Jesus say, *Lora, you did not need a man like that! It's okay to want that, but you do not NEED a man like that. You have me, and I will always be there for you. I will always hold your hand, and I will walk you home.*

My husband and I had worked out the details of the divorce and were ready to sign the papers. Then one morning, God woke me, and it was impressed upon me to call my husband and talk before I could sign the papers. So that is what I did. I knew I could not sign the divorce papers unless I did this. I did not know if he would even talk with me, but he did. Later that day, he came over to the house. We sat down to talk, and I asked him if he could tell me he had peace about the divorce. If he had peace about this and knew it was what he wanted, I could sign the papers and move on with my life. He said that he did not have peace. We decided to go to counseling and see if we could work things out. Through all of this, I never doubted that my husband loved me. If I did not think he loved me, I would not have been willing to try and repair our marriage.

Well, this was even more stressful than finding out about the affair. Over the next year, my husband would move back in to our home and leave again. He did not seem committed to our relationship. I felt in my heart that God wanted us together, but I could not deal with the stress of this relationship any longer. I prayed and told God that I was done. If He wanted this relationship to work, He would have to do something now. I was at the end of my rope, and I let go. Shortly after this, my husband called and said he wanted to move back into our home. He had a change of heart and really wanted to seriously work on our marriage. I told him if he wanted this to work, he would have to prove this to me. I had given all that I had to give. I had taken all of the hurt and rejection I could handle. He did this, and our relationship is better today because of all we went through. We appreciate each other more and no longer take each other for granted.

I learned to trust him again by trusting God through my husband. Later I asked him what happened that caused him to make up his mind to call me that day and recommit to our marriage. He said that he had a dream. In this dream, his dad, who passed away a couple of months after we separated, had an old classic truck he was driving. My father-in-law loved classic cars and was a member of a car club. He asked my husband to ride with him. They were driving and talking. My father-in-law asked my husband a question. He said,

"Son, are you just going to let Lora walk away?" My husband turned to look at his dad and his dad turned his head to look away. I believe this was a dream from God. It started my husband thinking that he did not want to lose me.

A couple of months after my husband and I reconciled, I found this new lump in my breast. At first, I was concerned but just talked myself out of the worry and told myself it was probably just scar tissue. Over the next couple of months, the mass was increasing in size. When I went to my doctor to get it checked, he was very concerned. He biopsied the area, and it was again breast cancer. He recommended to completely remove the breast. I decided to have both of my breasts removed since this was the third time I had dealt with this and I did not want to take the chance that I would develop cancer in the other breast. After I had surgery, I again started on chemotherapy. I tolerated the chemotherapy fairly well. I had the nausea and fatigue but not as severe as previously. I lost all of the hair on my head again. One of my patients gave me a beautiful wig to wear, and I made it through the recommended treatments. I was able to continue working through this in God's strength. A few months after the chemotherapy was complete, I started on the surgeries to reconstruct my breasts. I never imagined the process for reconstructing my breasts would take four years and multiple surgeries, but it did.

A year after the chemotherapy was completed, my PET scan showed a mass on my sacral bone. This bone is at the bottom of the spine. The doctors did not think it was cancer at first. They did a CAT scan of the area, and it was read as normal. Six months later, it was time for another scan, and I had changed doctors to go to someone closer to my home. My new doctor asked me if there was anything I was concerned about, and I told her about the mass on my sacrum. She ordered a special type of PET scan that would better look at the bones. This showed the mass had doubled in size from the previous scan. It was in an area that could not be biopsied. She started me on an oral chemotherapy. Three months later, the scan revealed the mass had not decreased in size, and it was causing pain. She recommended I see a radiation oncologist. He recommended fourteen radiation treatments. I completed the radiation treatments, and I have had no more problem in that area.

A few months later, my PET scan revealed an area under my right arm that was thought to be a lymph node. At first, they did not think it was cancer. I was having scans every three or four months to watch the area. My doctor said they were "stable." Then, after several scans, the area had increased in size; and my doctor recommended that I have the area frozen. It was located on top of a nerve. It was frozen and disappeared for a time. I was having a lot of negative effects from the oral chemotherapy; and my doctor recommended, since my scans were good, to stop the medication.

About two years later, the area returned and again under my right arm. My doctors watched it for several scans, and it began to cause a lot of pain down my arm. The doctors did not feel that freezing the area again was a good idea. They felt there could be more complications from the procedure and I could possibly lose the use of my arm. They thought they could only shrink the lesion and did not think they could resolve it. Radiating the area was also thought to be too risky.

The only option was to go back on oral chemotherapy. My doctor said that she would leave the decision up to me. She seemed to think that we could continue to watch the area. I had surgery scheduled for a problem that had developed as a result of the radiation I had to my pelvic area. A hole had formed in my bladder. My surgeon did not want me to start the chemotherapy until after the surgery. Before I could have the surgery, I had another PET scan which revealed another spot that lit up in my right neck area. I decided I should not wait until after the surgery and felt that I needed to go ahead and start the oral chemotherapy. My doctors said as long as my white cell counts stayed in a good range, I could have the surgery while on the chemotherapy. I was able to have the surgery, and it was successful at first. Then six weeks after the surgery, the problem recurred. I had a catheter placed in my bladder for several months to take pressure off of the hole until I could have a second surgery. Altogether I dealt with a catheter and leak in my bladder for about three years. It was a difficult time with frequent infections and a lot of antibiotics. The second surgery was successful, and I am so very grateful.

A few months after the bladder problem was resolved, my right arm began to have numbness, increased pain, and then weakness in my right hand. The initial nerve conduction study showed cubital tunnel syndrome. The only option was surgery. I had surgery to release the ulnar nerve at the elbow. I also had numbness in some of my fingers, and the surgeon suggested that he also do a carpal tunnel release at my wrist. I agreed. I was desperate for a solution. I am right-handed, and I was having difficulty writing. After the surgery, none of my symptoms improved. The pain, weakness, and numbness were progressing rapidly. I had another nerve conduction study which revealed the lesion was on the medial cord of my right brachial plexus nerve. I had surgery to remove the mass, which was successful. The lesion had wrapped around a nerve. It was the size of a fifty-cent piece.

The pathology report revealed no cancer. After the surgery, I did not improve, and my symptoms worsened. Another test was done which revealed the cause of my symptoms was on the middle and lower trunk of the brachial plexus. I underwent another surgery to remove scar tissue and lymph glands from around the nerves. I am currently still standing on God's Word and waiting for the full manifestation of my healing. I think it is very interesting that the symptoms of right arm and hand pain, weakness, and numbness started to drastically worsen as I began writing this book. I believe the right arm and hand symptoms are an attack from Satan to try and stop the writing of this book. I am determined that the enemy will not succeed in his attack against me, and I will do what God has for me to do.

Four months after the last surgery on the brachial plexus, I went to my surgeon for a follow-up of a thyroid nodule that I have had since 1999. The nodule was biopsied in 1999, and the pathology revealed that it was benign. The nodule has remained stable. Since it had been twenty years since the nodule was biopsied, my surgeon wanted to biopsy it again. This time, the pathology revealed papillary cancer. I had surgery to remove my thyroid gland and underwent radioactive iodine treatment. I will have to take thyroid hormone replacement for the rest of my life. I am grateful that the cancer was completely encapsulated and all of the surgical margins were clear.

God has carried me through this twenty-year journey so far, and I know He will continue. I continue to declare the Word of God is true, and I believe that His truth can change the facts. My body is a temple for the Lord, and cancer has no right to exist in my body. God is not a man, and He cannot lie. He loves me, and I am His. I declare that He will satisfy me with long life. I will do all the things He has for me to do, and when it is my time to go home, I believe I will know. In spite of all the negative reports I have had over the years, the feeling that I was going to die has never returned.

Through the years, I have used traditional methods and alternative medicine to stay well. I educated myself on nutritional medicine and became board certified in integrative medicine. I have used naturopathy, nutritional supplements, acupuncture, and other methods to compliment the medicines that my doctor recommended. I made changes in my diet also, and I strive to eat healthy every day.

We live in a fallen world. Bad things happen in our lives. These are just some of the things that have happened in my life to try and stop me from the will of God. But they have not been successful, and they will not be successful. No weapon formed against me shall prosper. A pastor friend of mine taught me a very important fact. When bad things happen, we have a choice. We can let the thing grind us down to a pulp, or we can choose to be stronger for having gone through the trial and allow God to do what He wants to do in our lives. I choose to be stronger for having gone through the trials. It is my prayer that something I have been through will encourage you and give you hope as you go through your trials. Don't accept what the enemy sends to destroy you as truth. The devil is a liar. God's Word is true. Use God's Word as medicine to all of your flesh.

God is limitless. He is almighty and more powerful than we can conceive. Don't set limits on what He can do in your life and what He can do through you. Just commit your life to Him and get ready for the awesome journey.

2

Inner Healing

One day after I had started on my healing process, I sat down on my sofa with my Bible in my lap and asked the Lord, *Why did this happen to me?* I opened my Bible, and it fell open to John 9:1–8 NIV:

> As he went along, he saw a man blind from birth. His disciples asked him, "Rabbi, who sinned, this man or his parents, that he was born blind?" "Neither this man nor his parents sinned," said Jesus, "but this happened so that the works of God might be displayed in him. As long as it is day, we must do the works of him who sent me. Night is coming, when no one can work. While I am in the world, I am the light of the world." After saying this, he spits on the ground, made some mud with the saliva, and put it on the man's eyes. "Go," he told him, "wash in the pool of Siloam" (this word means "Sent"). So the man went and washed, and came home seeing. His neighbors and those who had formerly seen him begging asked, "Isn't this the same man who used to sit and beg?" Some say that he was. Others said, "No, he only looks like him." But he himself insisted, "I am the man."

It is not about why things happen in our lives; it is about learning to lean on Jesus as we go on our journey. If we allow Him, God can take what the enemy sends to destroy us and bring good to our lives and others' lives. The important thing is not what happens in our lives, but what we allow God to do in us through the trials, that is important. He will strengthen us and heal us of our emotional wounds through the struggles in our lives. This is important because we are spirit, soul, and body. What happens to the physical body can affect the soul, and things that occur to our soul can affect our physical being.

God showed me a vision of a vase that had no bottom. It was at the bottom of a river with clear water. He showed me the inside of the vase, and there was no gravel or sand. It was perfectly clean, and there were no cracks in the vase. The water was flowing undisturbed through the top of the vase and out the bottom. God was showing me He wants us to be like the vase: free of gravel and sand with no cracks or holes. He wants the Holy Spirit to be able to flow through us to present His glory. If we have sand and gravel, the flow of His spirit gets disturbed; and if we have cracks, the flow of His spirit gets misdirected. He wants us to be able to pour out what He pours into us, but with our sand and gravel and our cracks, we cannot be the most effective vessels for him.

So what are our sand, gravel, and cracks? These are our emotional wounds such as hurt, resentment, bitterness, and fear. Our Heavenly Father wants to heal these wounds in us. A lot of us have a tendency to push these wounds down inside our soul and try to overcome the hurts in our lives. No matter how hard we try to overcome emotional wounds, they seem to resurface over and over again in our lives. Have you ever felt like you were going around in circles winding up in the same place over and over again? Have you ever felt like you were climbing the same mountain in life over and over? Well, I certainly have.

Our emotional wounds cause us to deal with things over and over again. God revealed to me that our emotional wounds are like abscesses. On the outside, everything looks fine until we come to that mountain or difficult situation and the emotional wound is revealed. If we let the skin heal over the abscess without cleaning out the pus, the abscess will eventually resurface. He wants to open our emotional abscesses and clean out the pus so we can heal from the inside out. If I see a patient with an abscess in the skin, it is very hard to anesthetize the area because of all the infection and inflammation in the skin. There is no way to open an abscess and remove the pus without pain. But the pain is momentary, and then the wound can heal from the inside out. God knows it hurts us to open up our wounds, but the hurt will only last a short time. And if the wound is truly healed, it will never resurface again.

I feel certain that most or all of us have emotional wounds. I was not aware of any emotional wounds in my life, but I felt that if there were any, I wanted them healed. I went to a ministry called Theophostic, which stands for the light of God. In this ministry, you allow God to reveal any lies you are believing and show you His truth. In one of these sessions, God revealed a memory of me when I was a young girl. I was polishing the furniture in my mother and father's bedroom. When I was done, I was so proud, and I went to my mother and asked her to come see. When she walked into the bedroom, she went to a large armoire where she found a streak of dust I had missed. I was so hurt and disappointed in myself. I told myself at that moment that nothing I did would ever be good enough. Then God revealed how over and over again that hurt and lie had resurfaced in my life. In school, a grade of 99 was not good enough. I would be disappointed with anything less than 100. I was striving for perfection because of this emotional wound. Perfection is demonic. No one but God is perfect. Who am I to think I could even come close to perfection? But I was striving for what I could never achieve. Therefore, I always felt like a failure and had very low self-esteem. This wound had caused a lot of unnecessary stress in my life. My mother had no idea I felt this way, and she loves me so very much. She would never intentionally want me to feel this way. The enemy took this situation and perverted it in my mind. Through one Theophostic session that day, He healed my wound and revealed to me His truth. I am good enough because He made me. He loves me just the way I am.

> I praise you because I am fearfully and won-
> derfully made; / your works are wonderful; / I
> know that full well. (Psalm 139:14 NIV)

This wound that had been in my soul for so many years was healed completely in a few minutes' time. God is so good. Only He could do this. I could have spent years in counseling trying to get over that one hurt. When I look back on that time, I feel sorry for the girl who stressed over unnecessary things, and I am grateful that God healed me.

In a subsequent session, I saw episodes of my life during which I felt the hurt of my father's disapproval flash like a movie screen in front of me. As fast as a memory came, I saw the hand of God with an eraser. He was erasing each one until the movie screen was white. I was a pleaser of people and equated approval with love. Each time I felt my father's disapproval, I equated this in my mind with being unloved. This was also a perversion of these events in my mind by the enemy. God took this lie from me and revealed to me how very much I am loved.

There was one session of this ministry in which I saw no memory. I just kept hearing these words over and over again like a broken record: "Let there therefore now be no condemnation. Let there, therefore, now be no condemnation. Let there therefore be no condemnation." In this Theophostic session, God showed me that I had forgiven others for the hurt they had caused me, but I had never forgiven myself. I had never thought about forgiving myself, and I did not know how. The counselor asked me how I was able to forgive others. I said, "Jesus in me helps me forgive others." Then the counselor told me the Jesus in me that helps me forgive others is not a respecter of persons. Just as Jesus helps me to forgive others, the Jesus in me can help me forgive myself. That day, I was healed of unforgiveness of myself. I felt so free. I have done other ministries for inner healing, and each time I have, God has been faithful to heal me and show me His truth. After each session, I have felt a little lighter and freer.

As we go through our journey here on earth, there are traumatic life events which could be anything from an offensive comment from another person to the death of a loved one. No matter how small these traumas are, they can affect our health and sense of wellness. These wounds can affect how we respond in different situations. I have had someone say something to me that extremely offended me, but I knew they were not trying to be hurtful. I had to do some soul-searching to try and understand why I was offended and ask God to forgive me and heal me. It was not what the person said. It was how I perceived what she said. God revealed to me that these emotional wounds can change our perception of what is said or done to us.

Someone may say to me, "Your shirt is pink." This should not be an offensive statement. However, when I was in middle school, I had been made fun of for wearing a pink dress and had an emotional wound from my past. I might be hurt by their comment.

It is not as much about the actual event as it is about how we perceive the event. Mind-body medicine studies have shown that if a person perceives the events in life as traumatic and detrimental, this can have a negative effect on their health. Likewise, if a person perceives the events of life as obstacles they can overcome, the events can strengthen their character. The same event would not affect their health negatively. Adults who perceived their childhood as stressful have a higher risk of cardiac disease than those who did not perceive their childhood as stressful.

These emotional wounds result from the hurts and traumas in our lives. These wounds may cause us to carry things such as bitterness, resentment, hatred, low self-esteem, jealousy, fear, depression, anxiety, and unforgiveness. These things change our perception of situations and circumstances. For example, if you were to correct someone with low self-esteem for doing something wrong and show them the right way to perform a task, they may become highly offended. However, if you were to correct someone with good self-esteem in the same manner, this person would be grateful to you for showing them the proper technique.

The deepest soul wound I have ever experienced was when my husband had an affair. I felt as if my soul had been ripped in half. God showed me a familiar scripture that I had memorized as a child, but I had never seen it this way before.

When I read Psalms 23:1–3 KJV: "The Lord is my shepherd; I shall not want. / He maketh me to lie down in green pastures: he leadeth me beside the still waters. / He restoreth my soul."

God stopped me right there, and the word *restoreth* leaped off of the page. He restores my soul! Hallelujah, I knew God was able to put me back together. He was going to carry me through and restore me. It was shortly after this that I awakened one morning and saw a vision of the hands of God with a needle and thread. He had my heart in His hands and was sewing my broken heart. No matter what we face, Father God is always there to heal us and strengthen us for every trial.

I believe if we are going to be the vessels for the Lord that we are called to be, inner healing is a must. God can still use us but not as effectively. One day during my quiet time, God showed me an ATM machine. I was at the ATM machine trying to withdraw some money from my bank account. The ATM had a sign on it that read "Out of Service." I felt very frustrated. I had put my money in the bank and wanted to get the money out right then so I could use it to purchase something. God said, *This is how I feel about you. I have put a lot of good things in you, and sometimes when I want to use you, I can't because you are 'out of service.'"* Our emotional wounds cause us to be out of service. When we heal those wounds, we can be more effective for the kingdom of God.

General prayer for soul-wound healing

Dear Heavenly Father, I forgive (whomever you need to forgive), and I repent of (sin). I ask You to forgive me for (what you have believed or done). I forgive myself for (sin). I command the spirit of (bitterness, resentment, depression, anxiety, abandonment, unforgiveness, hatred, jealousy, rejection, fear, etc., whichever spirits need to leave you) to go back to hell where they came from in Jesus's name and consider their assignment against me null and void in the eyes of God and of no account. I cancel all of the devil's power over me because of this (sin). I ask You, Father, to repair and reverse any damage done to me by these spirits. Holy Spirit, show me Your truth in Jesus's name. Amen.

3

Who We Are in Christ

Once the emotional wounds in our souls are healed, we can learn and accept who we are in Christ. We are spiritual beings who live in a body and have a soul. Our spirit is aligned with God when we accept Jesus as our savior. We line up our soul with our spirit by healing our emotional soul wounds and renewing our minds with the truth of God's Word.

> My son, attend to my words; incline thine ear unto my sayings. Let them not depart from thine eyes; keep them in the midst of thine heart. For they are life unto those that find them, and health to all their flesh. (Proverbs 4:20–22 KJV)

When we align our soul with our spirit, the physical body should come into alignment also.

We have to rebuke the lies that contradict the Word of God. We do not deny the facts; we simply know that the truth of God's Word can change the facts.

> We demolish arguments and every pretension that sets itself up against the knowledge of God, and we take captive every thought to make it obedient to Christ. (2 Corinthians 10:5 NIV)

Do not accept what man tells you, even doctors, as the absolute truth. God's Word is the absolute truth. God is not a man, and He cannot lie.

> God is not a man that he should lie, nor a son of man that he should repent. Has he not said and will he not do it? Or has he spoken, and will he not make it good? (Numbers 23:19 NIV)

> So that by two unchangeable things in which it is impossible for God to lie, we who have taken refuge would have strong encouragement to take hold of the hope set before us. (Hebrews 6:18 NIV)

> Also the Glory of Israel will not lie or change his mind; for he is not a man that he should change his mind. (Samuel 15:29 NIV)

> Now all glory to God, who is able, through his mighty power at work within us, to accomplish infinitely more than we might ask or think. (Ephesians 3:20 NLT)

God, through his power at work within us, is able to do more than we can conceive or imagine. Some people get instant miracles, which is wonderful. Some of us have to walk through the fire and trial. When we walk through the trials, God will be faithful to strengthen us and will always use our experiences for our good or to help others. We have a will. We have a choice. As we walk through the trial, we can let it beat us down and destroy us, or we can allow God to do what He wants to do in our lives and walk in our true identity in Him. He will make us stronger and better for having gone through the fire.

It takes faith to walk out a healing. I have thought over the years that I may not have enough faith for my healing. Then God showed me His truth.

> For by grace are ye saved through faith; and that not of yourselves: It is the gift of God. (Ephesians 2:8 KJV)

> For I say, through the grace given unto me, to every man that is among you, not to think of himself more highly than he ought to think; but to think soberly, according as God hath dealt to every man the measure of faith. (Romans 12:3 KJV)

Notice that Paul says *every* man, not *some* men. Also he says *the* measure of faith, not *a* measure of faith. Faith is a gift from God, not something you create. God gives each of us the measure of faith we need.

God may be waiting for a time to answer your prayer, but He always answers. It is not about you; it is about Jesus and what He did on the cross.

> He himself bore our sins in his body on the cross, so that we might die to sins and live for righteousness, by his wounds you have been healed. (1 Peter 2:24 NIV)

Not believing God will carry you through a trial has nothing to do with you not having enough faith. It is saying that what Jesus did on the cross was not good enough. Our confidence is found not in who we are but in who Jesus is and who we are in Him. In Jesus, we are the righteousness of God.

> God made him who had no sin to be sin for us, so that in him we might become the righteousness of God. (2 Corinthians 5:21 NIV)

I can do all things through Christ who
strengthens me. (Philippians 4:13 NKJV)

In Him, we can do all things. When I was going through the
separation from my husband, God brought this scripture to my mind
one day when I was doubting I could get through. And the word *all*
leapt out to me. I heard the Lord say, *All means all, even this.* In that
moment, His Word was all the reassurance that I needed. I know His
Word is true and He cannot lie, so I knew I could handle whatever
was in front of me with Him by my side.

With the strength of Christ, we put on the armor of God and
stand against the enemy.

Finally, be strong in the Lord and in his
mighty power. Put on the full armor of God, so
that you can take your stand against the devil's
schemes. For our struggle is not against flesh and
blood, but against the rulers, against the author-
ities, against the powers of this dark world and
against the spiritual forces of evil in the heavenly
realms. Therefore, put on the full armor of God
so that when the day of evil comes, you may be
able to stand your ground, and after you have
done everything, to stand. Stand firm then, with
the belt of truth buckled around your waist, with
the breastplate of righteousness in place, and with
your feet fitted with the readiness that comes
from the gospel of peace. In addition to all this,
take up the shield of faith, with which you can
extinguish all the flaming arrows of the evil one.
Take the helmet of salvation and the sword of
the Spirit, which is the word of God. (Ephesians
6:10–17 NIV)

Buckle the belt of truth around your waist. God's Word is the
absolute truth. Satan is the father of lies.

> You belong to your father, the devil, and you want to carry out your father's desires. He was a murderer from the beginning, not holding to the truth, for there is no truth in him. When he lies, he speaks his native language, for he is a liar and the father of lies. (John 8:44 NIV)

Anything that is contrary to the Word of God is a lie. We cannot deny the facts of the doctor's report, but when we walk in the supernatural realm with our belt of truth, we know that God's truth can change the facts. We have to rise above how we feel or how things look in the natural and stand on God's Word knowing we are healed by the stripes of Jesus. The breastplate of righteousness guards our heart and vital organs. It protects us from the condemnation and lies of the enemy. It is the righteousness of Jesus which we are freely given that protects us when we put on the breastplate.

> God made him who had no sin to be sin for us, so that in him we might become the righteousness of God. (2 Corinthians 5:21 NIV)

The helmet of salvation protects our minds from the devil's lies. When we are certain of our salvation and what we have in Jesus, we have a peace the enemy cannot steal. We put on our shoes of peace to help us walk like Jesus walked. The devil's mission is to do whatever he can to stop us from doing what God has called us to do. Our shoes of peace help us to not get tripped by the lies and obstacles the devil puts in our way on our journey to our destiny. Remembering that faith is a gift from God, we take the shield of faith with which we can block all of the fiery darts from the enemy. When the lies, temptations, and doubts come, we can quench them with our shield of faith. We take the sword of the Spirit which is the Word of God to defeat the devil and to protect ourselves just like Jesus did in the wilderness.

> Again, the devil taketh him up to an exceedingly high mountain, and sheweth him all the

kingdoms of the world, and the glory of them; And saith unto him, All these things will I give thee, if thou wilt fall down and worship me. Then saith Jesus unto him, get thee hence, Satan: for it is written, Thou shalt worship the Lord thy God, and him only shalt thou serve. Then the devil leaveth him, and, behold, angels came and ministered unto him. (Matthew 4:8–11 KJV)

For the word of God is quick, and powerful, and sharper than any two edged sword, piercing even unto the dividing asunder of soul and spirit, and of the joints and marrow, and is a discerner of the thoughts and intents of the heart. (Hebrews 4:12 KJV)

God's Word is our most powerful weapon. So be strong, victorious, mighty, powerful, righteous, and worthy. This is your identity in Christ.

The Power of the Blood

When I was a young girl, I learned to sing a song in church that boasts of the wonder-working power of the blood, the precious blood of the Lamb. It wasn't until years later that I realized I had no idea of the power about which I was singing.

> In whom we have redemption through his blood, the forgiveness of sins, according to the riches of his grace. (Ephesians 1:7 KJV)

The *New Living Translation* of this verse states: "He is so rich in kindness and grace that he purchased our freedom with the blood of his Son and forgave our sins."

The blood of Jesus is powerful enough to pay for all of our sins and grant us salvation. His blood is not only powerful enough to save us, it is also powerful enough to heal us.

> Christ redeemed us from the curse of the law by becoming a curse for us, for it is written: "Cursed is everyone who is hung on a pole." (Galatians 3:13 NIV)

The curse is sin, sickness, poverty, and anything bad.

> But He was wounded for our transgressions, He was bruised for our iniquities; the chas-

tisement of our peace was upon Him, and by His
stripes we are healed. (Isaiah 53:5 NKJV)

Some teach that this verse is only for spiritual and emotional healing. Well, I always look for things to make sense. My God is not a god
of confusion. He made our being, spirit, soul, and body. Why would He
heal our spirit and soul but not our body? If my child fell and scraped
her knee, I would not simply comfort her spirit and soul, I would also
attend to her physical wound. So if I have a physical problem, why
would God do any less for me, His child, than I would do for my child?

If you, then, though you are evil, know how
to give good gifts to your children, how much
more will your Father in heaven give good gifts to
those who ask him! (Matthew 7:11 NIV)

Everyone that is prayed for does not get healed. I do not understand this, but everyone who is prayed for does not get saved either.
God provided for everyone's salvation. He did not make hell for us.
That place is for Satan and his demons. It is not God's desire for anyone to not receive salvation, yet some are not saved. If salvation is for
everyone, why would healing not be for everyone?

But if we walk in the light as He is in the
light, we have fellowship with one another and
the blood of Jesus Christ His Son cleanses us from
all. If we say that we have no sin, then we deceive
ourselves, and the truth is not in us. If we confess
our sins, He is faithful and just to forgive us our
sins and to cleanse us from all unrighteousness.
(1 John 1:7–9 NKJV)

The blood of Jesus is also powerful enough to purify us from all
unrighteousness. That would be any unrighteous thoughts, unrighteous will, unrighteous emotions, and unrighteousness in our physical bodies. In the physical sense, our blood gives life to our bodies.

The blood takes oxygen and nourishment to all of our cells. It also removes toxins from our cells and takes them to our liver where they are processed for elimination. Toxins are also eliminated through the lungs, intestine, kidneys, lymph system, and skin. In the spiritual realm, the blood of Jesus gives us life. Spiritually, the blood of Jesus courses through our arteries bringing healing and life. His blood flows through our veins taking away toxins and disease. It cleanses us from all toxic thoughts, will, and emotions. It cleanses us from anything that is contrary to the truth and will of God. I believe it is not God's will for us to be sick; therefore, I believe this cleansing includes physical toxins and illness as well.

The blood of Jesus is so powerful it bought us complete and total access to God.

> Therefore, brethren, having boldness to enter the Holiest by the blood of Jesus, by a new and living way which He consecrated for us, through the veil, that is, His flesh, and having a High Priest over the house of God, let us draw near with a true heart in full assurance of faith, having our hearts sprinkled from an evil conscience, and our bodies washed with pure water. Let us hold fast the confession of our hope without wavering, for He who promised is faithful. (Hebrews 10:19–23 NKJV)

This passage tells us that we can boldly approach God by the blood of Jesus and ask that His will be done in our lives. In the Lord's Prayer, Jesus tells us to pray God's will be done here on earth as it is in heaven. There is no sickness in heaven! Hallelujah! So we can boldly ask Father for our body to be healed here on earth as it would be in heaven.

The blood of Jesus also provides protection.

> The blood will be a sign for you on the houses where you are; and when I see the blood,

> I will pass over you. No destructive plague will touch you when I strike Egypt. (Exodus 12:13 NIV)

In this scripture, the children of Israel had broken their covenant with God. Pharaoh refused to let God's people go, so God sent a plague to kill all the firstborn children. God's people were protected from this curse by applying the blood of a lamb over their doorposts. This blood is a symbol of the blood of Jesus who was slain from the foundation of the world. The blood had to be applied to the doorposts in order to protect the Israelites. Since this blood was a symbol of the blood of Jesus, we can also symbolically apply the blood of Jesus over ourselves and our families to protect us from anything evil which includes sickness and disease.

The blood of Jesus shed on the cross defeated the devil. We have victory over the enemy by the blood.

> They overcame him by the blood of the Lamb and by the word of their testimony. (Revelation 12:11 NIV)

There is nothing more powerful than the blood of Jesus. As we apply the blood of Jesus in our lives, we have power to defeat and overcome anything the enemy brings against us. The victory is ours by the blood of the Lamb!

5

His Word Is Medicine
to All of Our Flesh

> My son, attend to my words; incline thine
> ear unto my sayings. Let them not depart from
> thine eyes; keep them in the midst of thine heart.
> For they are life to those that find them, and
> health to all their flesh. (Proverbs 4:20–22 KJV)

The Hebrew word for heart in this scripture is *levavecha* which means "inner man and mind." The Hebrew word for health is *marpe* which means "a healing and cure." My interpretation of this scripture is "My child, pay attention to what I say and read aloud my words. Commit them to memory because they are a cure, medicine, to your body." So many people are quick to toss out God's Word as medicine when they read it once and do not get immediate results. But when we have an infection, it is rare to be able to take one dose of an antibiotic and be cured. We may have to take the medicine two or three times per day for ten days or longer to be cured. We do not take one dose and throw the rest away if we do not feel better after the first dose. Likewise, we may have to read healing scriptures two to three times per day for a period of time until we receive our healing. God's Word is the only medicine I am aware of which has no side effects, and you cannot overdose on it.

If a person has high blood pressure, he may need to take medication daily to keep the blood pressure under control. To keep ourselves well, we may need to read aloud healing scriptures daily. I have learned that maintaining my healing is a lot more difficult than getting well. Once we get to feeling better, we tend to slack off on our health maintenance practices. It is important to be diligent in our healthy practices every day. Our bodies are a product of what we do every day, and God has given us authority over our physical bodies. We cannot eat candy bars every day for breakfast, lunch, and dinner and expect to stay well. We have to nourish our bodies with daily physical and spiritual nutrition. Speaking God's truth over our bodies is just as important as eating our vegetables every day.

When we take medicine, our bodies have to digest the medication and apply it to the problem or sickness we are trying to cure. It is the same with God's Word. We have to digest or meditate on the Word and apply it to our problem. The Holy Spirit will guide you as to which scriptures and how often you should take them as medicine.

(A list of healing scriptures is included in this book as an addendum.)

Reading scripture is easy, but how do you digest it and apply it to your life? Faith comes by hearing the Word of God. So we must speak scripture aloud over ourselves and make it personal. If you cannot speak scripture over yourself, have someone else speak over you. Sometimes we have to speak the scripture or scriptures once, and sometimes we have to speak them several times every day. Just as some foods are harder to digest than others, so are some scriptures. Speak the scripture until you have the faith or until you feel release from the Holy Spirit. Then apply the scripture to yourself and your situation.

For example, 1 Peter 2:24 KJV says: "Who his own self bares our sins in his own body on the tree, that we, being dead to sins, should live unto righteousness: by whose stripes ye were healed."

To apply, this scripture to my life might read like this: Jesus paid the price for my sins on the cross. Therefore, I am dead to sin and alive unto God, and by the stripes of Jesus, I am healed.

Words can bless us or curse us. In Matthew 12:37KJV, Jesus said, "For by thy words thou shalt be justified, and by thy words thou shalt be condemned."

In Mark 11:23 KJV, Jesus said:

> "For verily I say unto you, that whosoever shall say unto this mountain, be thou removed, and be thou cast into the sea; and shall not doubt in his heart, but shall believe that those things which he saith shall come to pass; he shall have whatsoever he saith."

We have whatever we say. So if we take the diagnosis the doctor gives us, we can speak that over ourselves or we can speak God's Word over ourselves. We are not denying the facts of the doctor's diagnosis, just speaking God's truth over our body, believing His truth will change the facts. My doctor may say that I have cancer, but I do not receive that diagnosis. I do not deny the cancer exists, but it is not mine. I deny cancer's right to exist in my body. I am healed by the stripes of Jesus.

> Death and life are in the power of the tongue: and they that love it shall eat the fruit thereof. (Proverbs 18:21 KJV)

The saying "Sticks and stones can break my bones, but words will never hurt me" is simply not true. Words can hurt us much more than sticks and stones. A broken bone can mend in six weeks, but the effect of negative words spoken to us or about us can last a lifetime. Kids who are bullied in school with words such as *stupid* or *ugly* often have low self-esteem, which may last for many years even into adulthood. Things which are spoken about us whether by ourselves or by another can affect our relationship choices, our career choices, and many other areas of our lives. Negative words can affect our success in life. These words may cause us to tell ourselves we do not deserve a raise or promotion, so we never ask. Low self-esteem may cause a person to believe they are not good enough for that special someone's love or that they cannot succeed in college. We tend to choose the path we feel we deserve.

On the other hand, positive words can have just as much impact as negative words.

A scientist conducted an experiment in which he spoke negatively to water, and when the water was frozen, the crystals were in disarray and were ugly. Then he spoke positively to water, and when frozen, the water crystals were beautiful. While not very scientific, this experiment is very interesting since our bodies are 65 percent water.

I had a book when I was a little girl titled *The Little Engine That Could* by Watty Piper. This is a great story about the effects of optimism and speaking positive words. The little blue engine has to get a train full of toys to the children on the other side of a huge mountain. This is a seemingly impossible task for such a small engine. The little engine tells himself over and over, "I think I can. I think I can. I think I can." After several tries which were unsuccessful, the little engine gets over the mountain. He did not get over the mountain on the first try. But he did not give up. He continued to tell himself "I think I can" until he made it over the huge mountain. In our lives, we also have mountains to climb. We can speak God's truth regarding these mountains until we successfully get over the mountain just like the little engine.

> For verily I say unto you, that whosoever shall say unto this mountain, be thou removed, and be thou cast into the sea; and shall not doubt in his heart, but shall believe that those things which he saith shall come to pass; he shall have whatsoever he saith. (Mark 11:23 KJV)

Our words are important. We cannot speak God's truth one minute and then complain about how bad our problems are the next. This is much easier said than done. We just have to try our best every day and keep speaking God's truth. Fortunately, we have a Heavenly Father who is full of grace and mercy, and He is faithful to forgive us when we speak contrary to His truth.

One day, the Lord brought to my attention Psalms 103:1 KJV: "Bless the Lord, O my soul: and all that is within me, bless his holy name." The Lord asked me what "all that is within me" means.

Well, I thought, *we are body, soul, and spirit. Our spirit is lined up with God when we are saved, so it blesses the Lord always. We do not have to tell our spirit to bless the Lord. So "Bless the Lord, O my soul." What is left is our physical bodies. "All that is within me" is our physical bodies.*

It was an instant revelation. The lightbulb turned on in my brain. God is telling us to instruct our physical bodies to bless Him. A sick body does not bless the Father, but a well body does! We can speak to our bodies and command them to bless the Lord with wellness. I want to encourage you to speak God's truth over your physical body every day.

6

Stop Fighting a Battle
That Is Already Won

> But He was wounded for our transgres-
> sions, he was bruised for our iniquities: the chas-
> tisement of our peace was upon him; and with
> his stripes we are healed. (Isaiah 53:5 KJV)

This scripture tells us that the price for our healing has been paid and the battle has been fought and won. When the enemy attacks us with a life-threatening illness such as cancer, we start trying to fight for our lives. This is our human instinct. We start listening to everyone's opinions about what we should do and where we should go. It is easy to get overwhelmed with others' opinions—what we should eat and drink, which doctors we should go to, what supplements and medications we should take, and what exercise we should do. We start fighting the battle that Jesus has already won. What we should do instead is pray and get clear direction from the Lord and let Him direct our path to wellness.

> The steps of a good man are ordered by the
> Lord: and he delighteth in his way. (Psalm 37:23
> KJV)

All we have to do is pray and get directions from God and follow His path to our wellness. There is a battle we have to fight, but this is not it. The battle is in our mind. We pray and stand in faith and believe God is working on our behalf for our good and His glory until we receive the manifestation of our healing. If we prayed and instantly received, we would not have any problem. The problem is when we pray and we wait and wait and wait sometimes years for the manifestation. After time and not receiving, we can get worn down, and we start believing the lies of the enemy. These lies are thoughts such as *God does not love us, We do not deserve healing,* or *We are not good enough.* All of these statements are contrary to the Word of God. Satan attacks our minds with these lies which affect our emotions, and our emotions start to control what we do. The emotions of our soul will take us down the wrong path. We get in God's way by doing what we feel or think.

> Fight the good fight of faith, lay hold on eternal life, where unto thou art also called, and hast professed a good profession before many witnesses. (1 Timothy 6:12 KJV)

Our fight is to hold fast to our faith and the truth of God's Word. We have to stay in agreement with God's truth.

> Can two walk together, except they be agreed? (Amos 3:3 KJV)

We cannot be in agreement with Satan's lies and walk out our healing. Now, we do not have to deny facts. The facts of a path report are real. But God's Word is true, and His truth can change the facts. We just deny the facts as our absolute truth. We have to take every thought captive and test each thought against the truth of God's Word.

Satan will also use suffering to attempt to destroy our faith. We cannot allow how we feel to determine our truth. We have to fight the fight of faith and stand on God's truth no matter how we feel. This is difficult when your arm or leg hurts so bad you want to cut it off or when you do not have the energy to get out of bed or lift your head off of the pillow. Yet how we feel does not change God's Word. His Word is true. God is who He says He is. He is not a man, and He cannot lie. Do not let your feelings or how you feel determine what you think or believe. We have to learn to live beyond how we feel and not make decisions based on our feelings.

> Trust in the Lord with all your heart, and lean not on your own understanding; in all your ways acknowledge Him, and He shall direct your paths. Do not be wise in your own eyes; fear the Lord and depart from evil. (Proverbs 3:5–7 NKJV)

Our battle is not for our healing. That battle was fought and won many years ago. Our battle is to keep our mind, will, and emotions in line with God's truth about us. We can add power to our lives by agreeing with God, or we can weaken ourselves by agreeing with the lies of the enemy.

> And be not conformed to this world: but be ye transformed by the renewing of your mind, that ye may prove what is that good, and acceptable, and perfect, will of God. (Romans 12:2 KJV)

God's will is for us to be well. A sick body does not bless Him. When we walk in victory and wellness, God is pleased.

7

Order

> For we which have believed do enter into rest, as he said, As I have sworn in my wrath, if they shall enter into my rest: although the works were finished from the foundation of the world. (Hebrews 4:3 KJV)

I was flying home from a conference, and I heard that still voice of God in my spirit.

He said, *What is order?*

I said, *What is order, Father?"*

He said, *Obtaining right direction and entering rest—ORDER.*

Rest means to cease work or movement in order to relax, refresh oneself, recover strength, or to be placed or supported so as to stay in a specified position. To enter God's rest means to be supported by Him, to be in the place or specified position He has for us, and to be relaxed, refreshed, and strengthened—not stressed. The Greek word for rest is *anapausis* meaning "cessation and refreshment." When we cease our own works and lean on God, we are refreshed. In order to enter this rest, we must obtain God's right direction or position for our lives.

How do we obtain right direction? First, we believe. We believe God is who He says He is and He will do what He says He will do. We believe His Word is true. Then we trust Him and lean on Him to carry us through our trials instead of trying to get through in our own knowledge and strength. We pray and do what God says to do.

Trying to figure everything out can drain our energy and cause stress and unrest. Trusting in God for our direction and healing causes us to enter His rest. We have to get out of the works of the flesh doing what we think or feel and do what God shows us to do. If we are in God's perfect will for our lives, we will be at peace or rest. Resting does not mean we are not doing anything. It means in the middle of our going to the doctor, having surgery, taking treatments, or therapy, we are at peace. In the middle of our storm, we can be at rest.

> Jesus was in the stern, sleeping on a cushion. The disciples woke him and said to him, "Teacher, don't you care if we drown?" He got up, rebuked the wind and said to the waves, "Quiet! Be still!" Then the wind died down and it was completely calm. He said to his disciples, "Why are you so afraid? Do you still have no faith?" (Mark 4:38–40 NIV)

Jesus was resting in the midst of the storm. The disciples were afraid. We cannot be worrying about our health or circumstances and be in God's rest. But if we have faith, we can be at rest during our trials. Rest is not dependent on our situations or circumstances; it is a condition of the soul.

Just as worrying and not having faith stills our rest, so will disobedience. Rest requires trust and obedience.

> Thus also faith by itself, if it does not have works, is dead. (James 2:17 NKJV)

I have seen people over the years who would not go to the doctor or take medicine because they were believing God for their healing. They had faith but did not do anything with their faith. If God tells you not to go to the doctor or to stop your medicine, then absolutely do what He tells you. Otherwise, pray and get direction from God as to which doctor to see and take your medication until you are healed and no longer need it.

We can learn to be in God's rest or peace no matter our circumstances. Rest requires believing God is who He says He is, having faith that His Word is true and He will do what He says He will do, obtaining His directions for our circumstances, and following through in obedience doing what He has told us to do. His order for our lives produces rest.

We have to keep an open mind. His order for our lives may not look like what we think it should. Sometimes our situations get worse before they get better. We have to put aside any preconceived ideas we have and follow in the direction of God's peace.

As we stay in God's rest in the midst of our trials or difficult circumstances, we draw attention to Him. Our rest in Him is supernatural, and as others witness our peace in the midst of life's storms, they will be amazed. Our trust in God through our trials makes a bold statement about who we are in Him. It is by God's grace that we get through the challenges in our lives.

> And He said, "My presence will go with you, and I will give you rest." (Exodus 33:14 NKJV)

> This saith the Lord, Stand ye in the ways, and see, and ask for the old paths, where is the good way, and walk therein, and ye shall find rest for your souls. (Jeremiah 6:16 KJV)

8

Walking in Victory

We are not victims; we are victorious in Christ. What Jesus did on the cross was horrible for Him to suffer. He suffered greatly for us. He does not want us to suffer. He wants us to lay down the cross of our sufferings and put on our crowns of His righteousness and walk in victory.

One day, I was driving down the road singing an old hymn, "The Old Rugged Cross." I started singing the lyrics "So I'll cherish the old rugged cross, / till my trophies at last I lay down. / And I will cling to the old rugged cross, / and exchange it someday for a crown."

I heard the Lord speak to my spirit, *That's wrong.*

I said, *Lord, what do you mean? I have been singing this song since I was a young girl. It's a beautiful song.*

He said, *What I endured on the cross was horrible, but I did it for you so you would not have to suffer. That happened a long time ago. I do not want you to cling to the cross. You do not have to wait until you get to heaven to lay your burdens down and exchange them for a crown. I want you to leave your worries and burdens at the foot of the cross and pick up your crown today. I want you to walk in my victory today here on earth.*

As we walk out our destiny or calling here on earth, God will take us from victory to victory. If we allow God to do what He wants to do in and through us as we walk through the trials in our lives, He will take us from one glorious victory to the next.

> But we all, with unveiled face, beholding as
> in a mirror the glory of the Lord, are being trans-

56

> formed into the same image from glory to glory,
> just as by the Spirit of the Lord. (2 Corinthians
> 3:18 NKJV)

As we move from glory to glory and from victory to victory, God's supernatural power transforms us and takes us into our full purpose and destiny. The trials in our lives cause us to learn more about who we are in Christ and to accomplish all that we are called to do in our lives here on earth.

It's in the difficult, scary places that God allows where we discover our true destiny. God does not cause sickness or bad things to happen in our lives; but He will use them to mold, change, or direct us.

> Blessed is the one who perseveres under trial
> because, having stood the test, that person will
> receive the crown of life that the Lord has prom-
> ised to those who love him. (James 1:12 NIV)

God will be faithful and carry us through our trials to victory. He tells us this in scripture.

> For the Lord your God is the one who goes
> with you to fight for you against your enemies to
> give you victory. (Deuteronomy 20:4 NIV)

> For everyone born of God overcomes the
> world. This is the victory that has overcome the
> world, even our faith. (1 John 5:4 NIV)

Through these difficult situations in our lives, God extracts the characteristics within us that He wants to shine much like a cook extracts the flavor from spices. According to author and Indian cooking teacher Raghavan Kasper, a good cook can extract as many as eight different flavors from a single spice depending on how the spice is processed. He uses cumin as an example. If you use cumin seeds as they are, you get their distinctive spice flavor. When you grind the cumin seeds, the flavor is musky and earthy. Toasting the seeds produces a nutty aroma. The flavors are all quite different, but they started exactly the same. Each of us has, within our self, many flavors or characteristics that need to be developed or extracted in order for us to carry the aroma of God. According to 2 Corinthians 2:14, God desires us to spread the aroma of the knowledge of Him everywhere. This is each of our mission: to spread the aroma of God wherever we go.

If we are going to walk in victory, we cannot focus on our problems or how we feel. We have to elevate our minds to the supernatural knowledge of God's truth. We have to walk in the supernatural realm knowing God's truth supersedes our facts. His truth does not depend on how we feel or what the medical report states. His Word is true, and the victory is ours. The victory is ours here on earth. We do not have to wait until we get to heaven to be victorious. I will continue to speak God's truth over my life, and I will continue to walk out my healing one day at a time. God is supernatural and limitless. I am determined not to set limits on what God is able to do in my life, and I will continue to speak His truth over my life. On my healing journey, I have had some wonderful experiences with God, and I look forward to seeing God's complete healing manifest in my body here on earth.

ABOUT THE AUTHOR

A former naval officer, Lora Efaw is a retired family physician and doctor of integrative medicine who provided patient care for twenty-five years. She earned her medical degree from the Medical College of Georgia, now Augusta University, and completed residency training at Naval Hospital Jacksonville. Before retiring from practice in 2019, she owned and operated a successful Christian-based clinic in Tifton, Georgia, which focused on preventive care and nutritional medicine.

CPSIA information can be obtained
at www.ICGtesting.com
Printed in the USA
LVHW021203290921
699020LV00006B/344